"A Dog's Life: No Shenanigans!"

He has some really funny and thoughtful ideas and even though, by his own account, he has no formal training of any kind, his strip has great energy and lightness. As long as he truly loves what he is doing and keeps at it, he'll continue to improve while maintaining his own unique style. As Don Bluth told me one late, late night so very long ago, "The best teacher is 'roll up your sleeves.'" Way to go, Christopher.
-Jim George, former Disney animator. http://drawthedog.com

How often do you follow a dream with no preparation and no prior experience? That's what "A Dogs Life" is all about. One man following his dream to sit down and draw funnies. These humble beginnings will warm your heart and tickle your funny bone.
-Ben Taylor

I know "everyone has to start somewhere" but this is ridiculous.
-some guy hiding behind the internet

This book is dedicated to my wife, Marlene, who makes me feel like the best cartoonist in the world when she laughs at one of my comics.

If I could only have an audience of one,
I'd want it to be her.

Foreword

In 2009, Chris had been telling me that he would like to write a webcomic for awhile, but he wasn't an artist. I suggested that he post a notice at VCU, a local college with an excellent art program. He never did, so I thought he had given up the idea.

Flash forward to about a year later. When Chris told me that he was going to write a webcomic and draw it I thought that this was probably a flash in the pan endeavor. I mean, he had never drawn anything before! Add to that the unfinished novel, the unlearned guitar and several other unfinished and abandoned projects; what was a girl to think? I was supportive anyway, found money in our budget for the web hosting, domain name, and art supplies and encouraged his first (very rough) drawings.

His first drawings were recognizable, but not much else; but the writing was funny! I laughed at almost every strip he showed me, and I knew that the drawing would improve with time. Now, almost two years later, he has developed his own style and his drawings are much more than recognizable; they look like an artist drew them.

I'm still a little surprised that he has stuck with it this long, but I'm very proud of him!

I hope you enjoy this book as much as I've enjoyed watching Chris grow as a cartoonist. I know it will make you laugh, even if you don't own a dog!

Marlene Otto

Introduction

Thank you for allowing me a moment to introduce myself and my comic! If you're a long time reader of "A Dog's Life", feel free to skip this part and jump right into the comics, although there may be some stuff in here that you didn't know about me.

I've been a fan of comic strips for as long as I can remember, and I think I always wanted to be a cartoonist, although I didn't realize it until recently. In elementary school, second or third grade, I think, I got in trouble for tracing "Peanuts" comics and selling them to the other kids for a nickel apiece. Later on, in fifth and sixth grade, my notebooks and book covers were littered with doodles of TIE Fighters, X-Wings, and Vipers from "Battlestar Galactica". In high school, I moved on to "Bloom County", and my notebooks were full of Opus and Bill the Cat scribbles. Somewhere along the line, I stopped doodling and simply enjoyed reading comics (probably after I got out of school and had no more notebooks or boring classes). Comic books, comic strips, I read a ton. When comics started showing up on the internet, I started in on them as well. I remember reading Penny Arcade, PvP, and Sheldon back in the "stone age" of web comics. As the years went by, my list of bookmarked web comics grew larger. I'd spend at least an hour every day after work tearing through them.

I've always dabbled in writing. I have many short stories and unfinished screenplays and one almost finished novel sitting in the file cabinet. In August of 2010, seeking a creative outlet, I thought it'd be neat to write a web comic. I came up with a few strip ideas about my dog and wrote them down. Once I started, the *need* to have a comic of my own grew into a raging fire in my head. I didn't want to go through the process of finding someone to draw my ideas, so, for the first time since in over 20 years, I grabbed a pencil, bought some sketch pads, and started drawing. I went to the Small Press Expo in Maryland in September of that year to buy "How To Make Webcomics" from my favorite cartoonist, Dave Kellett, creator of "Sheldon". Dave is really the guy who inspired me to get off my butt and make my own comic; "Sheldon" is such a fantastic comic. I wanted to create something that might make other people as happy as much as his comic makes me happy. I got home, tore through that book, drew up about 30 strips in a week and a half, purchased a domain and hosting, and started posting comics.

This remains my only real regret about this entire endeavor. I am quite proud of the writing in my early days, but the art is just not good (in my opinion). The fact that I got people to read it, and keep reading it, still makes me both shocked and pleased. I started up a Facebook fan page and an ad with the credit that came with my hosting plan. I will never forget the first time some-one "Liked" the comic on Facebook that was not a friend (if you're reading this, hiya, Chevy!). That was when I realized that, although creating the comic was really for me, I had the ability to make other people smile at my little scribbles as well. That was when this little hobby of mine became a passion, something that drove me to continually work on improving my drawing and writing.

This book contains most of the comics from my first year as a cartoonist. Another book will have the rest, "Bark To The Future", guest written by Ben Taylor, who I met while volunteering at the Virginia Comicon. Have fun meeting the characters and watching my art evolve with just about every strip. I hope you enjoy this collection, and be sure to keep up with Hunter and his pals at http://adogslifecomic.com

My first year as a cartoonist was full of great experiences; getting mentioned at "Draw The Dog", my first convention, selling my first sketch, and watching my art evolve into something that people would actually pay money for. I'm still learning and improving all the time, and striving toward that dream of turning this hobby into an actual career. It may never happen, but I'll keep reaching for it.

I'd like to take one more moment to thank:

Ben Taylor and Matt Carroll for teaching me the ins and outs of conventions from an insider's point of view. They've both been great friends and insanely supportive of the comic and myself. Ben has also written over a year's worth of strips in our "Bark To The Future" story and never asked for a dime.

Matt and Shawn Fillbach for tons of inspiration, support, and being awesome artists and friends.

Brett Carreras (brettscomicpile.com), "retired" promoter of the VA Comicon for giving me a shot and being a truly amazing supporter of the comic.

And, of course, *you, dear reader*. Either here or online, the thought of you reading my stuff and enjoying it fills me with a joy that is indescribable with mere words.

Hunter S. Thompson is a handsome chocolate labrador. He is very smart, able to learn commands quickly and open doors, but pretty dumb at the same time (he falls for the fake throw every dang time). Loves eating, fetch, chewing things up, Diane, and Jack...probably in that order.

Gillian McLean is the newest member of the family. She was adopted from a local agency after spending her puppy months in a kennel and then bouncing around a few foster homes. Her last foster home was an underground Doggy Fight Club, where she got her scars. She enjoys hoarding toys, although she doesn't play with them. She is extremely grateful to be in a real home with a last name. She became fast friends with the spider in her crate, and is able to speak many other species' languages, which she learned as a pup in the kennel.

Jack and Diane McLean are Hunter and Gillian's people. They do their best to take care of their dogs, but are somewhat oblivious to what they're really up to.

Boris the Spider lived under the chair until he was almost vacuumed up. He now lives in Gillian's crate. We know very little about Boris, apart from the fact he apparently knows dog commands, complete with the hand motions.

Gunter S. Thompson is Hunter's twin from an evil "mirror Earth". His goal is to send Hunter back to the evil world and take his place here, so he can play fetch and get belly rubs. Oh, also to keep existence from getting wiped out across all realities.
But mainly for the belly rubs.

Brodie is one of the dogs that Gillian lived with before getting adopted. He runs some sort of doggy fight club, although it seems to be more practice than actual fighting. Brodie is just mean, through and through, although he needs a bigger dog to hide behind.

Frances, a.k.a. Flunky, also lived with Gillian at the foster home. Frances isn't the smartest dog around, and she follows Brodie's orders without question. Deep down, all she really wants is puppies.

Frohike the crazy squirrel lives in a tree in the McLean's back yard. Full of conspiracy theories, he wears a tinfoil hat to keep the aliens..or was it the government…whatever…out of his brain. Dreads the coming of the Fat Cats who are taking over the world. We're talking twenty pounders, man.

This was the idea that started it all! I was thinking about making a comic about Hunter, and this strip popped into my head, just as you see it; albeit drawn in my head much better than it was actually drawn. In my excitement to start posting comics, my art was my biggest weakness.

Second comic drawn, and I already resort to the cheap groin shot joke. An important thing to note about this strip is the first appearance of Boris the Spider. I drew him in there as a throwaway joke to show how rarely we clean under furniture. I had no idea he would evolve into a regular character in the strip.

Very soon after we brought him home, it became clear that Hunter was going to be a big dog. His paws were HUGE. Abnormally so. It was always fun to watch him trying to run around, as he would invariably trip himself up on his too big for his little puppy body paws. The strip is just a slight exaggeration.

The start of my "story of the week" format. I tried to write out strips so that you'd have a short little story line running Monday, Wednesday, and Friday, then something different on Sunday. This is based on the true story of crate training Hunter. As you will see, we were far from successful. This strip would eventually be used for a dog training blog, much to my excitement! You can read some great crate training tips at http://www.workingk9-5.com/2012/04/crate-training.html along with other tips and tricks on raising up that puppy right. Also of note, this is the first full appearance of the "man" and "woman" characters. I usually only drew their feet for a good reason, folks....

Part 2 of crate training week. I wish it was this easy to get Hunter into his crate when he was a puppy. He was NOT a fan of the crate.

Another only *slightly* exaggerated true story. When we tried to crate train Hunter, he really did bark for a good hour before we gave in. He has not been in the crate since.

Hunter got into his locked food bin once by pulling the door off it's hinges after he found he couldn't pull the lock off. He did stop eating....eventually. His belly was noticeable larger. We never actually tried the "let him eat until he's full" thing, as it was clear we'd have one fat puppy if we did.

Panel one: true. Panel two: also true. Panel 3: not so much, although it'd be pretty cool! I got the idea into my head that dogs can read books by chewing them up, with interesting gastric consequences. Hunter was very partial to those Alex Cross books.

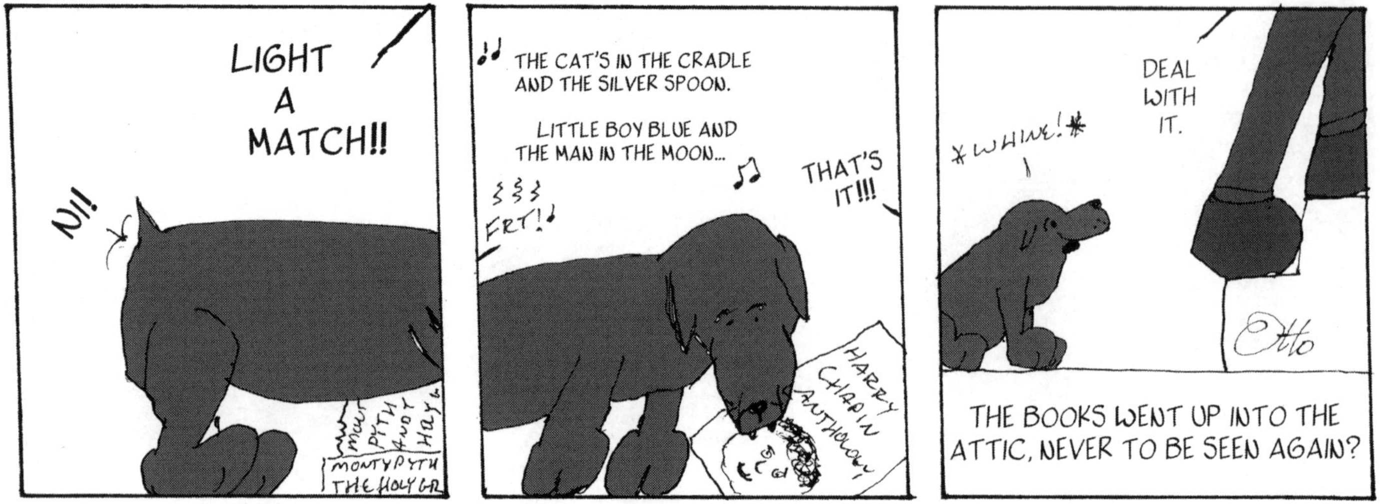
NI!
LIGHT A MATCH!!
MONTY PYTH THE HOLY GR
THE CAT'S IN THE CRADLE AND THE SILVER SPOON.
LITTLE BOY BLUE AND THE MAN IN THE MOON...
FRT!
THAT'S IT!!!
HARRY CHAPIN ANTHOLOGY
WHINE!
DEAL WITH IT.
THE BOOKS WENT UP INTO THE ATTIC, NEVER TO BE SEEN AGAIN?

There *will* be more "dogs eating books" comics. Not in this book, but after "Bark To The Future" for sure.

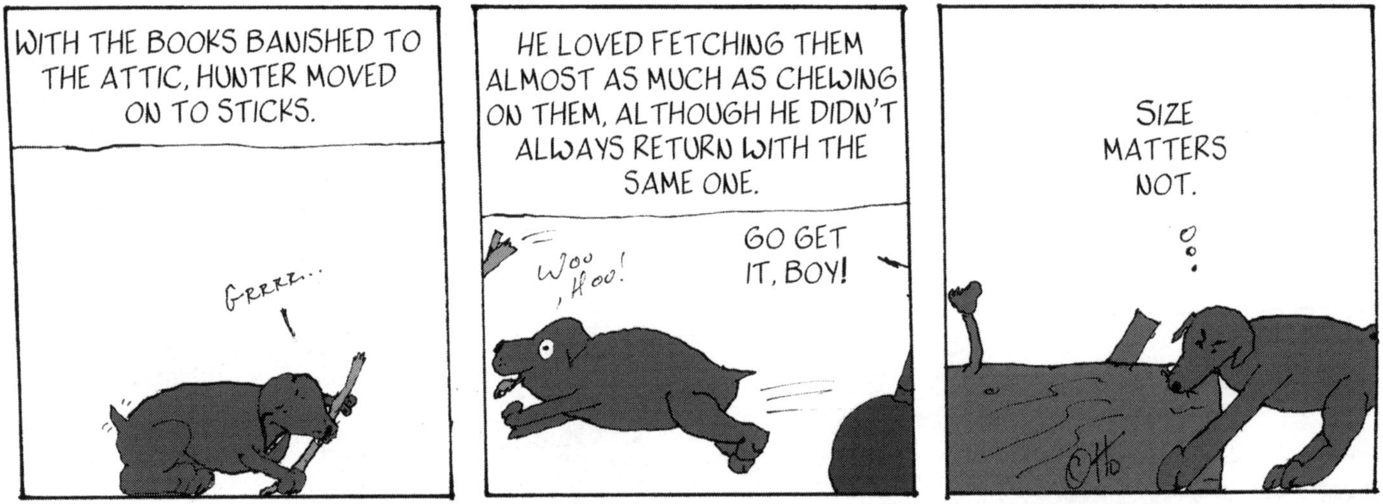
WITH THE BOOKS BANISHED TO THE ATTIC, HUNTER MOVED ON TO STICKS.
GRRRR...
HE LOVED FETCHING THEM ALMOST AS MUCH AS CHEWING ON THEM, ALTHOUGH HE DIDN'T ALWAYS RETURN WITH THE SAME ONE.
Woo, Hoo!
GO GET IT, BOY!
SIZE MATTERS NOT.

Based on a true story. Hunter found a branch about three times longer than himself and dragged it around for weeks. Also of note, my first geeky pop culture reference; a Yoda quote. This is the first strip of what I ended up calling "sticks week". You'll see why.

I originally envisioned doing the strip just like the comics in the paper that I grew up on; shorter black and white strips during the week, and a double sized full color one on Sunday. I eventually went full color during the week, and the double sized Sunday strip lasted close to a year. Unfortunately, I had to cut back to three strips a week because I just didn't have the time to keep it up. This strip is, as many of the strips are, based on a true story. We had a cat door in the back door that led to a screened in porch, where Hunter would go to the bathroom. It was just a matter of time before he out grew it, but he kept going through as long as he could. When he essentially became a contortion artist to get through it, we upgraded to a bigger pet door. It was pretty funny watching him squeeze his big ol' body through that tiny door though. I'm a cruel, cruel man. "We're gonna need a bigger door" is an homage to one of my favorite lines from "Jaws", one of my favorite films. "We're gonna need a bigger boat."

Hunter still falls for the fake throw. Not as often, but you can catch him off guard every now and then. After three or four fake throws, he starts getting frustrated. Again, I am a cruel, cruel man.

Two Star Wars references in one week! I'm a huge Star Wars fan, which becomes pretty evident as the strip goes on. Yes, I have an original 12" Boba Fett action figure, and no, Hunter never chewed it up. He'd have gone to the pound if he had. And not the nice pound either, he'd go to the pound that was on 60 Minutes*. And there's Boris again! This strip is where I got the inkling of turning the spider into a character.
*joke stolen from Dan Casey.

Of all my early strips, this is the one I am most proud of, I think. An 80's style training montage, complete with red headband! I especially liked the slightly nervous look on Hunter's face on the "Heel!" panel; he never really took to the leash and heeling.

I changed the woman character to a redhead, because I felt having both human characters with black hair would be visually dull.

Hunter was very easy to train. Unfortunately we haven't kept up with all of it and he can be a little crazy at times, as many labs are. All in all, he's a good dog, though.

Another week, another story line. This is the strip where Boris starts to become an actual character in the strip. And, of course, Hunter is scared of the vacuum, as many dogs are. I've done a few vacuum jokes, and I'm sure I'll do more.

Would Hunter bark at and chase a spider? Heck yeah. Would he ever actually catch one? Heck no. In this strip, we begin to see that Boris is no ordinary spider.

Boris finds himself a new home! Since Hunter doesn't go in the crate, he should be safe and sound there. I enjoyed drawing that first panel from Boris' perspective. Also, I switched fonts in this strip, to one a little more simple. Apart from my "hand lettering phase", I use this font as my main text in every strip.

As I mentioned at the beginning of this book, I started posting comics after only drawing for about two weeks. I regret that decision to this day, but at least I could joke about it. I still have issues with consistency in sizing things, but not as bad as I did with drawing Jack's feet in those early strips.

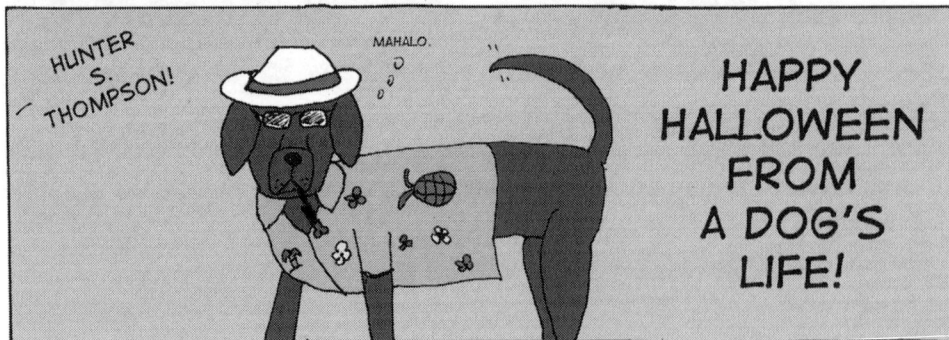

My first holiday themed comic! I had fun drawing Hunter in different outfits, especially as his namesake, Hunter S. Thompson. I drew Jack in a kilt because I also have a kilt and it is my favorite thing to wear. I just wish I had more opportunities to wear it!

"Arrrrrrrf" still cracks me up.

Another true story. Have I mentioned that I am a cruel, cruel man?

Hunter really did try to eat that pepper for a good little while, barking at it every time he spat it out.

I came up with this idea while watching the 2010 Yankees/Rangers postseason series. By the time I sat down to draw it, much to my chagrin, I had to add "The Rangers Win" to that last panel. Ah well.

I made myself giggle with the thought of Hunter "digging in" at the plate. The rest of the team petting him and saying "good boy" also makes me smile.

This is the strip that begins the "adopting Gillian" story line. You may notice the font is my old one; this strip was actually done, scanned, and colored a couple of weeks before posting. I didn't want to go right into the Gillian story, so I came up with a few strips to pad things out before adding a new character.

I was never able to train Hunter to do this. He got the unicycle riding down, but he can't juggle more than three balls.

My Yankee fandom, if in question after the dream strip, is strengthened in this strip with that Derek Jeter shirt.

Hunter loves him a car ride. He loves sticking his head out the window, and his jowls usually puff up like a parachute. I swear I get worse gas mileage when he's riding with me.

In this strip I tried to get across the idea that dogs don't understand everything we say, but they certainly know many words and phrases. Whenever you say "want" to Hunter, he gets all perky eared and wags his tail. He knows good things are coming.

I liked the idea of Hunter meeting several dogs at the adoption clinic. Augustus is named for Augustus Gloop from "Charlie and the Chocolate Factory" by Roald Dahl. Fantastic book and movie. I even liked the Johnny Depp one. I feel really bad for poor Augustus. aw.

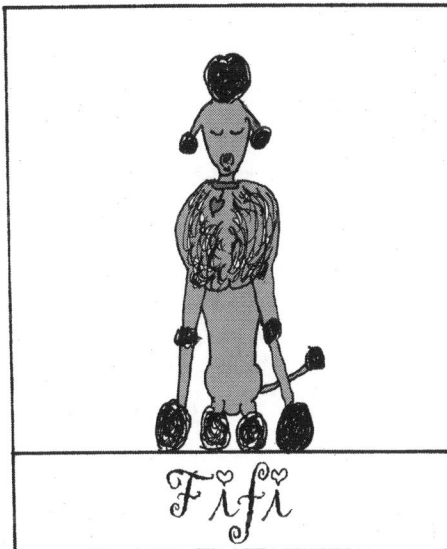

My attempt at making Hunter look suave, slicking his fur back and grinning. I personally think I failed miserably.

Here we see that Hunter is not a fan of little yip-yip dogs. This is also based on reality. Dang little yip-yip dogs; they think they're so big and tough.

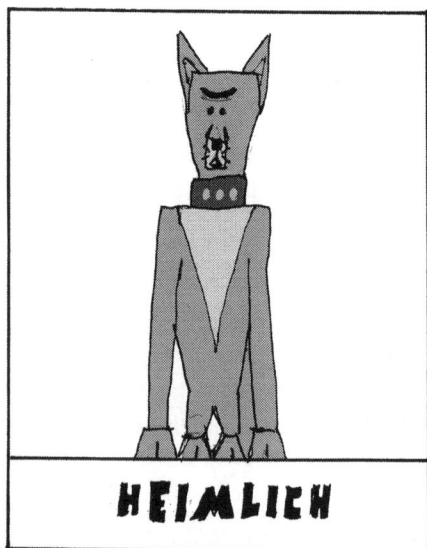

Fun fact; "Nein!" and "Achtung!" are pretty much all the German words I know.

SWIFFER

IS IT A DOG OR A DUSTMOP?!

DUNNO. I

SNIFF SNIFF

AM I SNIFFING THE RIGHT END?

SNIFF

This strip actually looked much better in the sketch book. I drew the dust pile too big, I think.
Fun fact; my wife came up with the punch line. I originally wrote it as "a dog or a dirt pile?" Dustmop is funnier.

WHO DESTROYED MY FAVORITE LAMP?!

NOT ME

It was totally the dog.

Filler strip! I envisioned myself occasionally drawing parodies or homages to other comics in the papers or online, as of this writing, this is the only one I have done so far. Not to say I won't ever do another one, but I just haven't gotten an idea for another one yet.

Actually, that's not true. I do have a good idea for one, but I need to improve my drawing skills before I try it. Think "Rex Morgan, M.D." or "Judge Parker". You know, those serial strips where nothing really happens for days at a time? I have a good idea for something like that.

Anyhoo...my parody of "Family Circus".

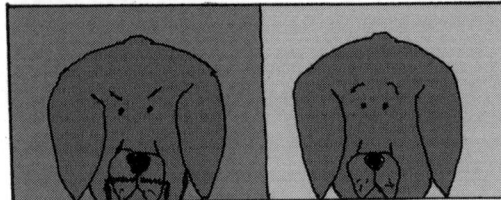

Lots happening in this strip! Mainly, of course, we meet Gillian, who will become Hunter's adopted sister and join him in his adventures and shenanigans.

Almost as important, we get the first glimpse of Hunter's evil twin. This was another case like Boris; I originally was just going to draw Hunter with a goatee just once as an "evil twin" joke. It's based on the original Star Trek series episode with the mirror dimension where evil Spock has a goatee. I quickly decided to make him a major character in the strip.

The real Gillian won us over pretty much as quickly as comic Gillian does. I was instantly smitten by her. She is the sweetest dog ever.

Adopt a rescue dog; they'll love you for it!

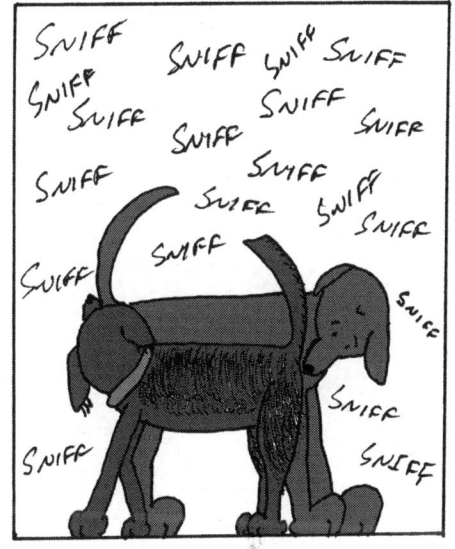

I like the idea that dogs just do doggy things like sniff butts and kick their leg when you scratch their bellies because we expect them to.

One thing I intended to get into more detail with but haven't gotten around to yet is the fact that Gillian likes to steal things. She is very quiet and sneaky, and likes to take Hunter's toys from time to time. We'll get more into her foster home soon. The real Gillian has a scar that she got at her foster home; I do not know if it was because she steals toys.

This was fun to write, with the dual conversations going on. Rubber Chickens was the funniest thing I could come up with for Jack to smuggle while keeping the strip "family friendly".

The first rule of Doggy Fight Club: You do not talk about Doggy Fight Club!

Yup....we'll be seeing Hunter's evil twin again!

The first appearance of Brodie the dachshund and Flunky (Frances) the bulldog! I like to think that dogs at adoption clinics really look forward to the day that they get adopted, because then they get a last name! Fun fact: Brodie is based on our friend Michelle's dachshund of the same name. He is the only dog I have ever come across that doesn't like me. He's not a mean dog, he eventually will tolerate me petting him after treat bribes and a couple of hours, but he barks and snaps at me every time we go to Michelle's place. It bums me out. Dogs usually warm up to me right away.

I tried to show how Gillian is a thief in this strip with her crate full of tennis balls. We also start to get the sense that Gillian's foster home is not a happy place.

Comics that take place at night are easy to draw.

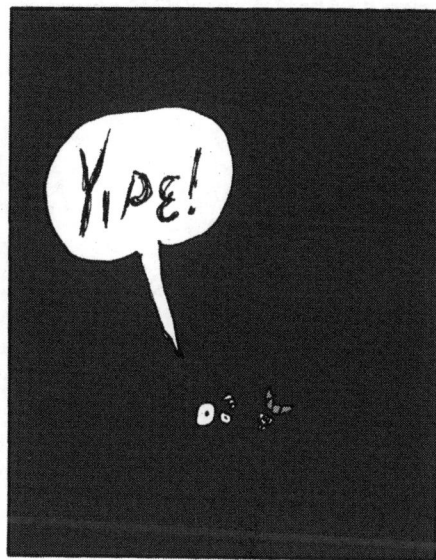

Quickest comic I ever drew. I should do more night scenes. Poor Gillian gets another scar.

Poor dim witted Flunky. She means well.

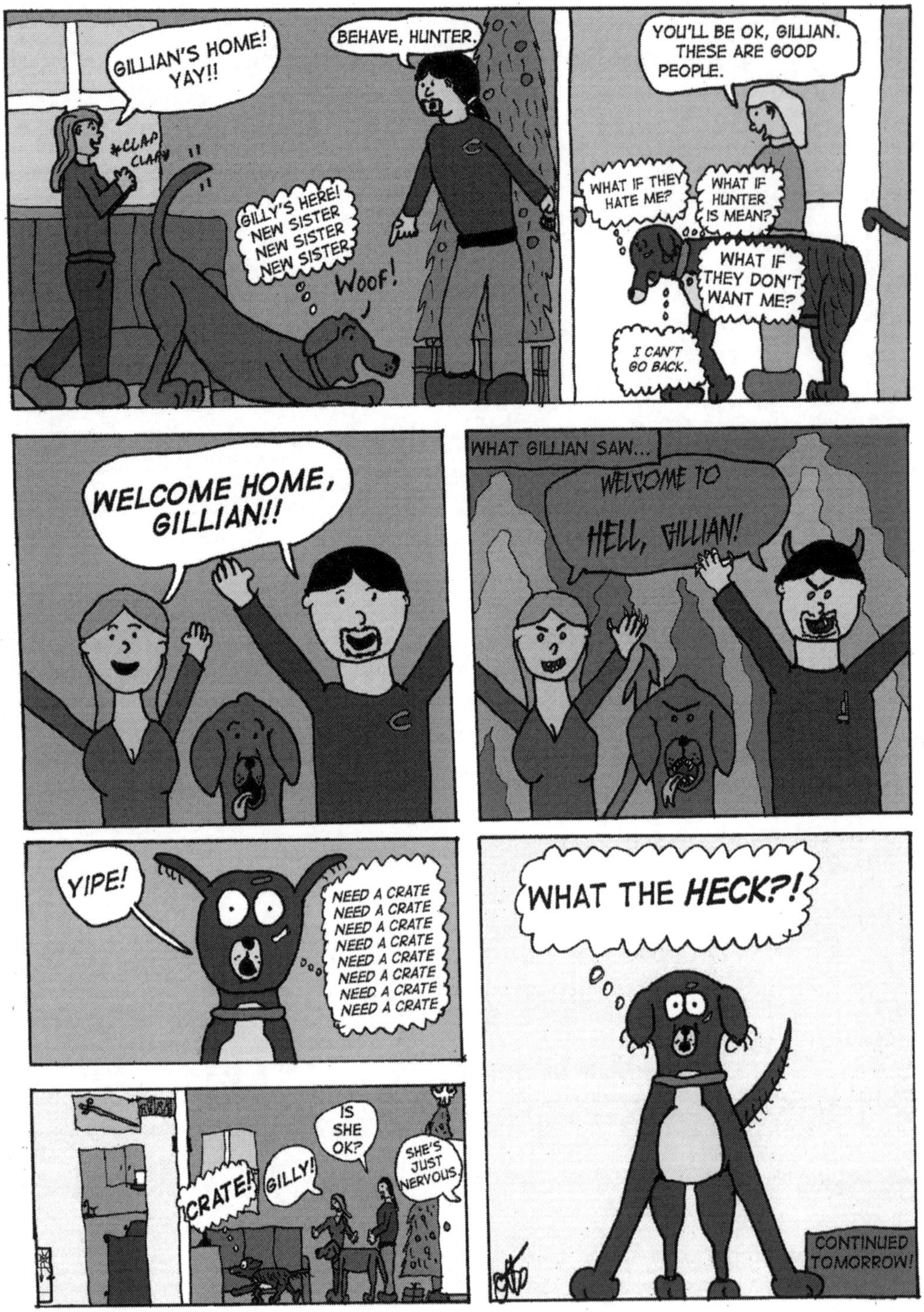
GILLIAN'S HOME! YAY!!
BEHAVE, HUNTER.
GILLY'S HERE! NEW SISTER NEW SISTER NEW SISTER
Woof!
YOU'LL BE OK, GILLIAN. THESE ARE GOOD PEOPLE.
WHAT IF THEY HATE ME?
WHAT IF HUNTER IS MEAN?
WHAT IF THEY DON'T WANT ME?
I CAN'T GO BACK.
WELCOME HOME, GILLIAN!!
WHAT GILLIAN SAW...
WELCOME TO HELL, GILLIAN!
YIPE!
NEED A CRATE NEED A CRATE NEED A CRATE NEED A CRATE NEED A CRATE NEED A CRATE NEED A CRATE NEED A CRATE
CRATE!
GILLY!
IS SHE OK?
SHE'S JUST NERVOUS.
WHAT THE *HECK?!*
CONTINUED TOMORROW!

I really had fun with this strip. Lots of little details! I especially get a kick out of the vacuum on Jack's sweatshirt in the "hell" panel.

Gillian has led a traumatic life and doesn't warm up to people right away. When we first got her, she spent a lot of time in the crate and her tail didn't come out from between her legs for a few days. I'll never forget the first time I saw her wag it! She's very sweet and loving now. I've said it before, and I'll say it again; adopted dogs are really some of the sweetest dogs you'll ever meet!

I came up with the idea that different animals speak different languages in the comic for one specific joke, which I haven't written as of this book's publication. It's kind of a pain to write sometimes, but it opens up a lot of fun options. Gillian speaks a lot of other animals' languages. Someday I'll write Gillian's origin story, like I did with Hunter (later on in this book!).

Fun fact: Boris got his name from the song by The Who, "Boris The Spider".

Hunter hates the vacuum with a passion.

I was so proud of that tennis balls/neutered joke. Pushing it for a family friendly strip, but sometimes a joke is too good not to write.

Gillian really doesn't like to play fetch. Hunter loves it enough for both of them, though.

This is the first strip where I mention a name for the humans. I named them McLean for Clan McLean, the Scottish clan I have ancestral ties to. At this point, I had not given them first names yet.

I really love that last panel. Gillian gets her name, and Hunter gets a frisbee!

More on the whole language thing in this strip. I also got to play around a bit with Boris in the background, getting himself some dinner.

Panel 1: YOU SEE THIS BUMP? / om nom nom / YOU GOT DROPPED ON YOUR HEAD AS A PUPPY?

Panel 2: NO! IT'S A "SMART BUMP!" / burp! / IT'S PRETTY BIG!

Panel 3: *FROM SPIDERESE / THE BIGGER THE BUMP, THE SMARTER THE DOG. / *HE'S REALLY NOT ALL THAT SMART. / snort!

I've read that that bump on the top of a dog's head is an indicator as to how smart they are. Hunter has a *huge* smart bump. Gillian's is kinda small, but she's pretty smart in the comic. In real life, not so much. Hunter is very smart, but also kind of dumb. In short; a Lab.

Panel 4: I CAN OPEN DOORS. I KNOW SOME TRICKS. I WAS TOP DOG IN OBEDIENCE SCHOOL... / HUP! / SO, HOW SMART ARE YOU?

Panel 5: I KNOW ALL SORTS OF PEOPLE WORDS. I CAN HEAR AND SMELL STUFF FROM / I CAN SPEAK SPIDER, SQUIRREL, CHIPMUNK, MOUSE, MOLE, VOLE, SEVERAL DIALECTS OF INSECT, BIRD, AND A LITTLE CAT.

Panel 6: WHERE THE HECK IS *YOUR* SMART BUMP?! / AAAND, I CAN "SIT"!

To be fair, he was the *only* dog in obedience school.

Fun fact! "Hup!" is my homage to Matt and Shawn Fillbach, talented artists and writers that I met while working at the Virginia Comicon in 2010. http://www.fillbachbros.com

My strip for new years day, 2011. Hunter is drinking Guinness. The real Hunter also likes beer, but don't worry, I don't let him drink. People are going to be reporting me to the ASPCA after reading this book!

It took a few days to get Gillian relaxed when we got her. Food always helped.

Our dogs are very good at "wait". They have pretty good willpower.

Fun fact! I hate drawing hands. Okay, not so fun, but definitely a fact.

A cautionary tale. If your dog is a large breed, don't let them on your bed when they are all small and cute. You *will* lose all your bed space. The "running dream" is very cute when he's sleeping on the floor, not so much when you take a paw to the chin at four AM.

This strip was the first time I used either of the humans' names in the strip, although I updated the cast page with their full names around the time I posted the Christmas strip with "Gillian McLean" in it. I named them Jack and Diane, because there's a comic in that somewhere. I haven't written it yet, but it's there, creeping about in my head somewhere....

Fun Fact! Another "Jaws" homage in that last panel.

Hey! There's the book title! Every time we leave the house, we tell the dogs, "No shenanigans!". Shenanigans are usually had.

The most common shenanigan we find is clothes on the floor. I'm pretty sure they grab them because they smell like us, but I have no way of being sure. I think this is my first "dogs have no concept of time" joke. I use this joke a lot. Perhaps too often, but I like it.

I like to imagine this is actually what they do with the clothes. In case you weren't sure, Hunter is talking about baseball. I guess that's how a dog would describe it.

This strip still makes me laugh out loud. The art in many of these older strips often makes me cringe, but I stand by the writing on every one. I'll stop patting myself on the back now.

Do dogs live in constant fear of the monster in the closet? When we open the closet door it must be torture on Hunter, because that's where we keep both the vacuum *and* his fetch stuff. Drawing Hunter's tail coming out of the fly on the jeans made me smile.

Hunter quickly learned how to open the door on the screened in back porch. I have forgotten how many different things I did to keep him locked inside. I think the thing that ended up working best was propping a ladder across it held in place with cinder blocks.

Gillian really does love to run. She doesn't play very much, but she does love a good game of chase.

Another "dogs can't tell time" joke. As I said earlier, I use this a lot, and it cracks me up every time.

The logs are under the porch because my friend Wendy thinks the way I draw logs is hilarious. Pretty much any time you see a random log drawn in somewhere in the strip, it's for her. That's friendship!

Hup!

The first appearance of Frohike, the conspiracy nut squirrel with the tin foil hat.

Not a boxer! See what I did there? I crack myself up.

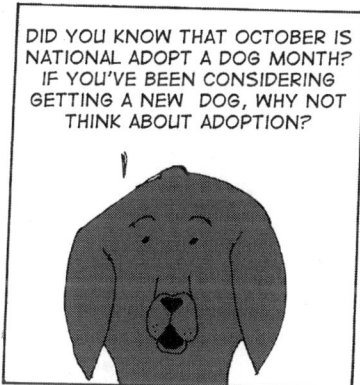

Another filler strip from early on. I put this up in October 2010 for National Adopt A Dog Month.

Here we find out that Hunter, for such a large, loud dog, is actually kind of a wimp.

For the record, I stole, "Listen! Do you smell something?" from Ghostbusters. That line always cracks me up.

Yip-yip dogs.....grrrr.

I remember getting kind of tired of drawing chain link fences at this point.

Poor Hunter....so dumb for such a smart dog.

I'm not sure why I drew Hunter looking like he had been decapitated. Ugh.

The little dog is Quincy, who is based on my friend Wendy's dog. Yup, the friend who likes the logs. Love ya, Wendy!

Really getting tired of drawing chain link now. You'd think I'd give myself a break, being the writer and all.

Poor Gillian, she has no idea they aren't supposed to be out.

I honestly think that this is how Hunter thinks. I've seen him trying to get at something he's not supposed to, moving very slowly, as if I'm not going to notice it if he goes slow enough.

If I had a nickel for every time I've said, "Hunter, I will end you", I'd have a whole lot of nickels.

Ahhh, the puppy dog eyes. Hunter breaks out the big guns. Don't ask me why Jack is so short in this panel, I have no idea what I was thinking.

DOGS DRINKING MARGARITAS

On the previous page....
"Works every time!" It sure does.

Dogs Drinking Margaritas stemmed from a conversation at a friend's birthday dinner during which, of course, margaritas were consumed. I forget exactly how it came up, but I went home and drew this up based on that classic work of art, "Dogs Playing Poker".

On this page; poor Gillian, she has no idea what a belly rub is, or what that involuntary leg twitch is that dogs get when you hit "the spot". I guess the second rule of Doggy Fight Club was, "never expose your belly".

Snarling dogs are hard to draw....

Here we get a glimpse of what Gillian's life was like growing up. Poor dog. I feel real bad for dogs that don't have a happy puppyhood. If I could adopt them all, I would!

Researching how to write "He's tickling my mouth" as if there was a spider in your mouth was unpleasant. I used a small spider. It did not tickle.

I wrote all these "spider in the mouth" strips just to set up what comes next.

Another story based on the truth. Gillian is a poo eater. At least we don't have to do much cleaning in the yard.

Not sure that there's too many predators for dogs to worry about in the suburbs....

If you go and look at the strips online, this is where I decided to try my hand at lettering by hand. I cleaned the text up for the book. The hand lettering didn't last long, I still need more practice, but I'd like to try it again someday. I envy cartoonists who hand letter well.

Gillian *loves* belly rubs now. You can't walk past her without her rolling onto her back and kicking back a leg to expose that belly for rubbin'.

Until we got the back yard fenced in, the dogs used the screened in porch as their bathroom. I didn't always get it cleaned right away; what I didn't get to, Gillian did. I've seen Hunter try it once or twice, but he doesn't do it often.

Another strip trying to show that Hunter is just a little too smart for his own good.
Fun fact! The only thing I dislike drawing more than hands or chain link fences; screened in porches.

The people from AARF, where we adopted Gillian from, actually did have it in our contract that we fence in the yard, and they did check up on it once or twice. We got it done on time (barely), and I always wondered what would have happened if we didn't. Were they going to repossess the dog?

The second appearance of the crazy squirrel, and more damn chain link!

In his lifetime, Hunter has figured out how to open the food bin, the inner front door, the back door, and both gates on our fence. There's always a way.

I never realized how much chain link fence there was in the world until I started drawing comics.

Another true story. Hunter barked at a weed for at least ten minutes; we have no idea what set him off. It must have moved. He has also barked at rocks, himself (in the mirror), and countless other phantom sights and sounds.

"Weedbarker" cracks me up. I like to think dogs have their own set of insults for each other. Our water dish really is that big.

I got the idea for this strip from a story that was told at church one morning. A single daffodil survived a late frost and our lay leader used it to convey that we, like that flower, can also survive through adversity. Ironically, she picked the flower and brought it to church with her.
This is the strip where I went back to the font instead of hand lettering.

This is a ritual in our house. We shower, Hunter rubs up against us as much as he can. Guess he likes us to smell dirty, or at least doggy. I decided to go without color for a couple of weeks while I worked on my coloring skills in Photoshop.

This was a quick story to have some fun with the local minor league baseball team's mascot, Nutzy, the Flying Squirrel. I like to think in the offseason he flies around the city, passively-agressively threatening dogs. He's a muscle bound rodent with a creepy smile, but he's fun to watch at the games!

NUTZY AND "HAVE FUNN" ARE © MINOR LEAGUE BASEBALL AND THE RICHMOND FLYING SQUIRRELS.

NUTZY AND "HAVE FUNN" ARE © MINOR LEAGUE BASEBALL AND THE RICHMOND FLYING SQUIRRELS.

We've never been to "Bark In The Park". Hunter would be uncontrollable, and Gillian would just freak out, I think.

Lots of fun little things in this strip. The "Steve" thing is from a Flight of the Conchords song. I wanted to name the squirrel after one of the Lone Gunmen from "The X-Files", and Frohike was the funniest sounding one. And, Gillian's "you said mutt" makes me giggle.

Naturally, a conspiracy nut squirrel's biggest fear is going to be cats trying to take over the world, right?

This is so true. The dogs love going out in the rain, but hate getting baths with the hose.

Just having finished up a longish story with Hunter's evil twin (later in this book) and knowing I had two long stories coming up ("Hunter's Origin" and "Bark To The Future"), I felt like drawing a few one or two shot simple joke comics. I wanted to give the readers a little break before diving into long stories.

Gillian is a *very* furry dog and sheds a **TON**. I don't like the fact that I don't have the artistic skill to draw her as furry as she actually is. Someday I'll get there.

Such a clown, that Gillian.

Hunter doesn't seem to have much of a sense of humor. I have to agree with him on that one though.... that's one lame joke.

One more strip before I dove into the longer stories....I had to deal with the fact that there was a chipmunk just chilling out at the dogs' feet.

I hadn't used the "dogs can't tell time" thing in a while. I felt it was due.

I loved drawing those tiny puppies.

Hunter is a big boy, and eats a lot. I imagine he did when he was a puppy as well.

Remember that strip earlier when Gillian asked Hunter if he was dropped on his head as a puppy? She was right!

And the smart bump is explained.

The guy we got Hunter from had a lot of dogs, including a super hyper Jack Russell terrier. He had all his legs, though. I got the idea for a side story about this three legged guy based on that terrier.

Ah, Hunter's disdain for lame jokes started early. Did I mention that I loved drawing those little puppies?

I had made a little running gag with the yellow lab who's always asleep. I love those fun little side gags.

I would think the wild dogs really dislike domesticated ones. Either that, or they're just jealous.

Ha! No corner is so tough that I can't write myself out of it!!!

Monty's a tough dog; I wonder why Hunter is such a wuss?

Filler! I had planned to put most of the filler stuff at the end of the book, but I've had to toss a couple in here and there to avoid blank pages in the book. I hope to get Stan to sign the original of this strip at the Baltimore Comic Con this year (2012).

I should've gone back and put scars on Monty in the earlier strips. Someday I'll get around to it....

I'm pretty sure this is the first time I drew a dog in 3/4 perspective. Up until now, they were always drawn from the side or straight on. I start to do it a little more often from here on out.

Panel 1: POOR TRIPOD! ANYWAY, AFTER HE FINISHED HIS STORY, WE MET JACK AND DIANE FOR THE FIRST TIME...

WHOA, WHOA...WHAT ABOUT THE OTHER DOGS?!

Panel 2: OTHER DOGS?

YOU SAID THERE WERE *LOTS OF* DOGS. *THEY MUST* HAVE STORIES!

IT WOULD TAKE **MONTHS** TO TALK ABOUT THEM ALL!

Panel 3: NO JOKE. **MONTHS!**

WHAT IS HE LOOKING AT?

I'm pretty sure this is the first time I broke the fourth wall (having the characters speak directly to the reader) apart from the "Adopt A Dog" and "Home Improvements" strips. You'll see the "Home Improvements" one later in this book.

Panel 4: I'LL NEVER FORGET THE FIRST TIME I MET OUR PEOPLE...

THEY. ARE. **SOOOO** *CUTE!!!*

Panel 5: IT WAS LOVE AT FIRST SIGHT!

LOOK AT THAT YELLOW SLEEPING ON BELLA'S BACK! *AWWWW!*

ZZZ...

PICK ME, PICK ME!

YIPE, YIPE!

RAR RAR!

PICK ME!

GRRR...

STOP IT!

©2011 ADOGSLIFECOMIC.COM

Panel 6: FOR ME, ANYWAY...

I HAD A YELLOW LAB GROWING UP, HER NAME WAS GILLIAN.

YAWN!

I WANT THIS ONE!

HRN!

I'LL GET YOU!

YIPE! PICK ME!

RAR RAR!

NO! PICK ME!

Hunter was not our first choice when we met the puppies. We wanted a chocolate female. You'll see how we ended up with Hunter soon.

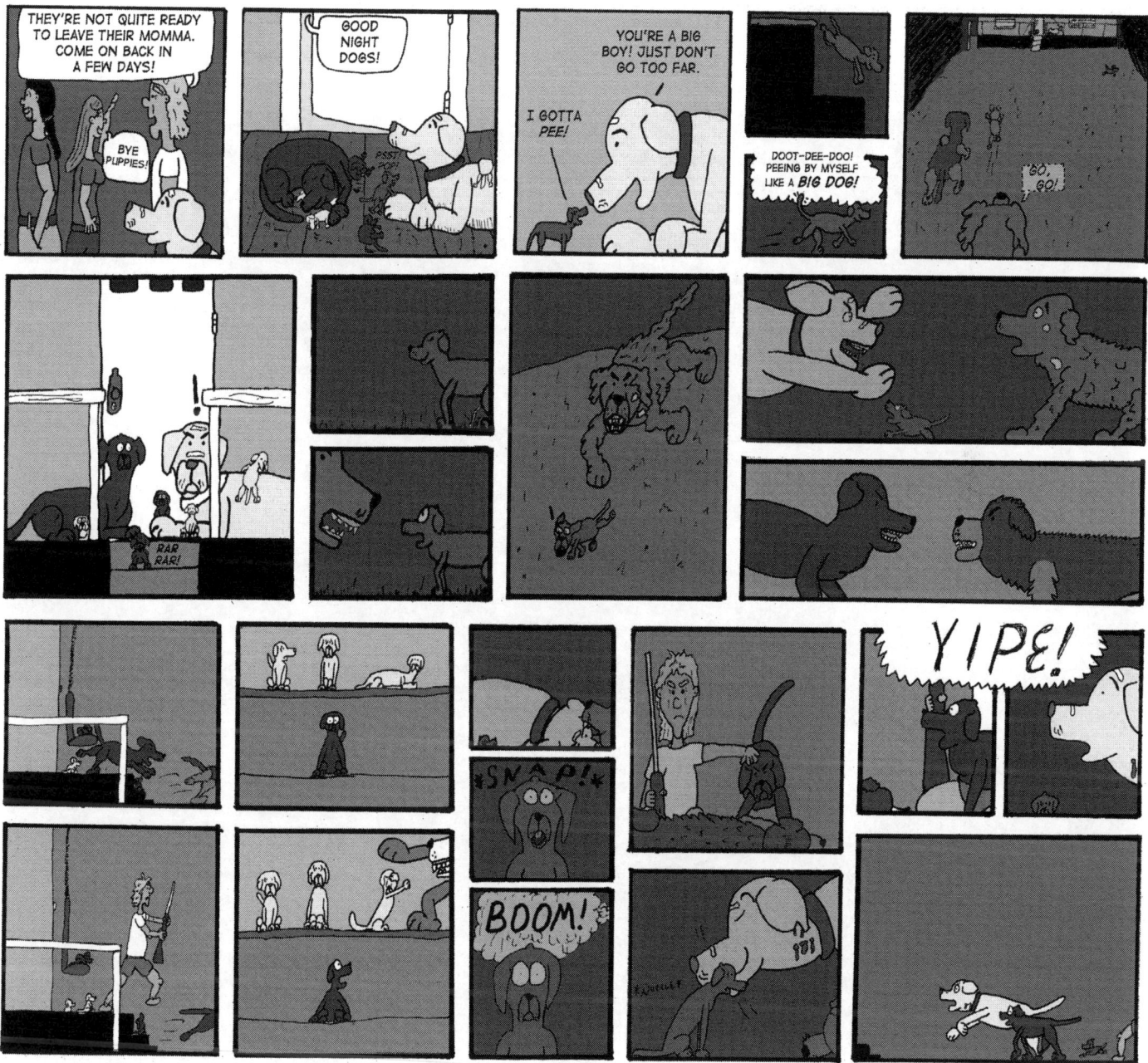

This might explain why Hunter's such a wuss. I would be too if some scary dog attacked me while I was peeing in the dark at night. I wanted to challenge myself artistically by finishing out this story with little to no words.

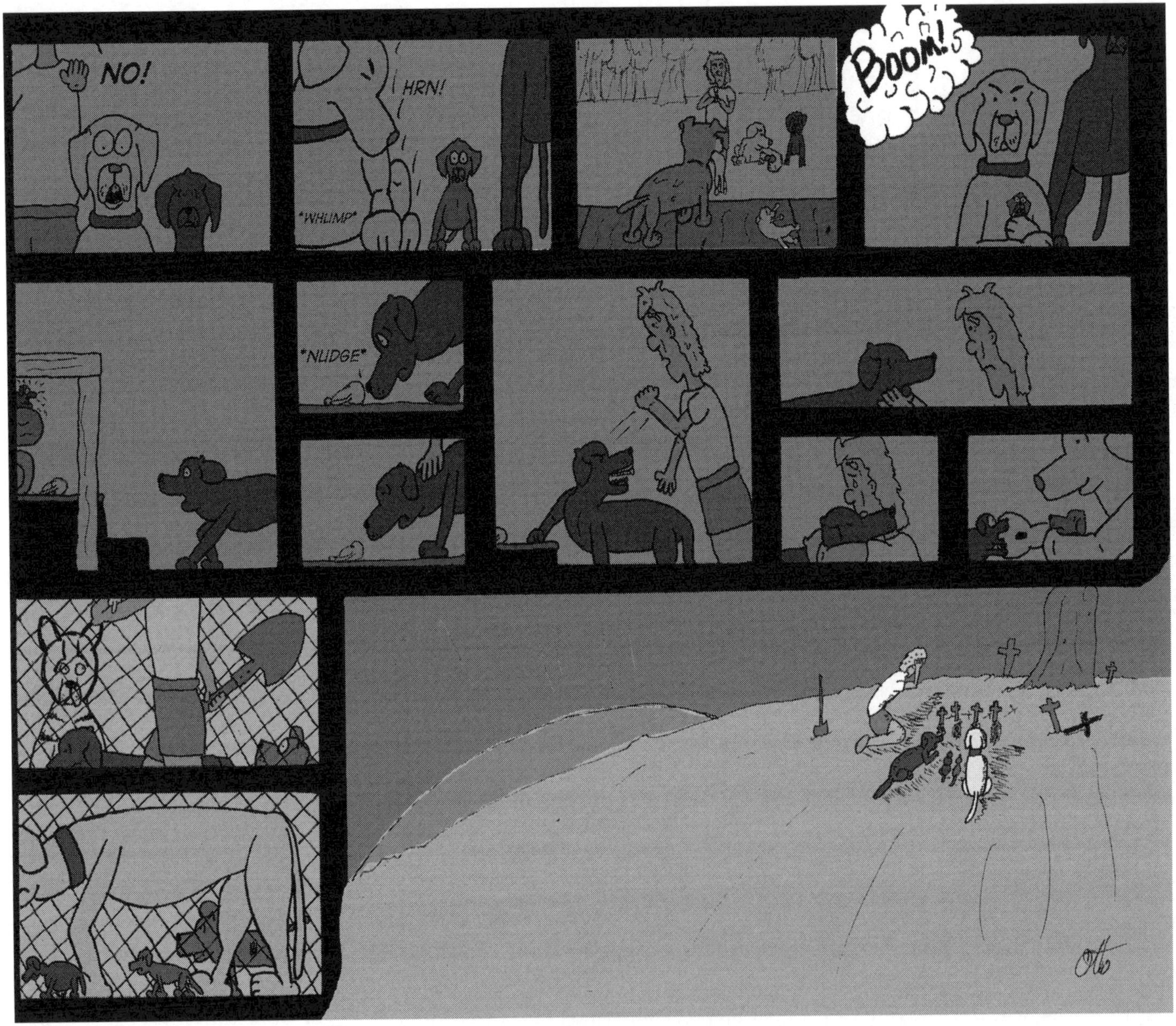
NO!
HRN!
WHUMP
BOOM!
NUDGE

I still get a little wet in the eyes when I look at these strips.

So, that's how we ended up with Hunter. Most of his siblings were killed by wild dogs. His brother went to my boss' neighbors, and we got him. I was sad when I heard about the other puppies, but we are so blessed with our boy Hunter. He's such a wonderful dog.

I liked ending the story here with a couple of nods to early strips. Peeing on the paper (strip one), and the car ride pose from the beginning of the "adopting Gillian" story.

I'm going to miss those little puppies; they were awful fun to draw.

The next several pages contain the story of Gunter, Hunter's evil twin, and Flunky and Brodie, Gillian's old house mates at the Doggy Fight Club foster home.

The first bunch were my Sunday strips, and then the others were done on Mondays during "Bark To The Future". I figured since I could put the book together however I wanted, I would put all his strips together for easier reading.

This is where we learn that Flunky's name is actually Frances. I hoped that between that and the pink collar, people would get that Flunky is a she. This becomes more evident in a couple of strips.

I love the idea of a dog from an evil earth wanting to just be a dog, while still being just a little evil.

I really wanted to show Gunter back on his evil home world just so I could draw Diane with a goatee. I also got to show that Gunter really just wants to be a dog. It's not his fault he's from an evil earth.

Aw. Poor Gunter. Even though they were evil, he still misses his people. Sadly, this is true for a lot of dogs. They just want to love their people, no matter how horribly they may be treated.

I really like writing for Frohike.

GUNTER'S STORY CONTINUES...
HOW IS A SQUIRREL AN EXPERT ON THE LAWS OF TRANSDIMENSIONAL TRAVEL?
HE USED BIG WORDS!
AND, HE WORE A SHINY TINFOIL HAT. HE LOOKED SMART.
SO, WHAT'S YOUR BIG PLAN, THEN?
I'M GOING TO BUILD A NEW...
TRANSDIMENSION RIFT OPENING MACHINE!!!
WE'LL NEED A CARDBOARD BOX, A ROLL OF TIN FOIL, AND A LOT OF USED DRYER SHEETS.
USED DRYER SHEETS?
THEY ABSORB STATIC. IT'S FOR THE SUPER ELECTRO-STATIC FIELD.
SCIENCE!
SERIOUSLY?

Science!!!

Frances falling for Gunter just sort of happened, unplanned. I plan on having a lot of fun with that side story.

Turns out Brodie out-evils the dog from the evil Earth. Maybe he comes from there, too.

Panel 1: AT GILLIAN'S OLD FOSTER HOME...

I BET I'M THE NICEST CAT AROUND IN THIS "EVIL EARTH" OF YOURS!

NOPE.

Panel 2: WHAT DO YOU MEAN, "NOPE"?! I'M EVIL! I CLAW FURNITURE AND FRAME BRODIE! *EVIL!* I GUTTED A CHIPMUNK JUST TO WATCH IT DIE! *EVIL!* A MIRROR WORLD ME WOULD BE ALL... *PURRING AND SNUGGLES!!*

NOPE.

Panel 3: IT DOESN'T MATTER WHAT UNIVERSE YOU'RE IN... CATS ARE *ALWAYS EVIL!*

Gunter's plan begins. Dryer sheets. **Science!**

These four strips ran during "Bark To The Future" on Mondays. It spawned a print that I sell at conventions, the "Evil Cat" print. I like cats, I've had them all my life, but let's face facts; they're evil. They're all purring and wanting petting, then, BAM, they bite you. They are ruthless killers of birds and rodents.

NO MATTER WHAT UNIVERSE YOU'RE IN...

CATS ARE

EVIL!

ADOGSLIFECOMIC.COM

Fun with Frances' crush. She's so cute and subtle.

This one was fun. I originally planned to have Brodie just cover Gunter's goatee with his paws, then decided a scribbly drawing would be more fun. I also debated on that last line...Rin Tin Tin? Lassie? Benji sounded funniest.

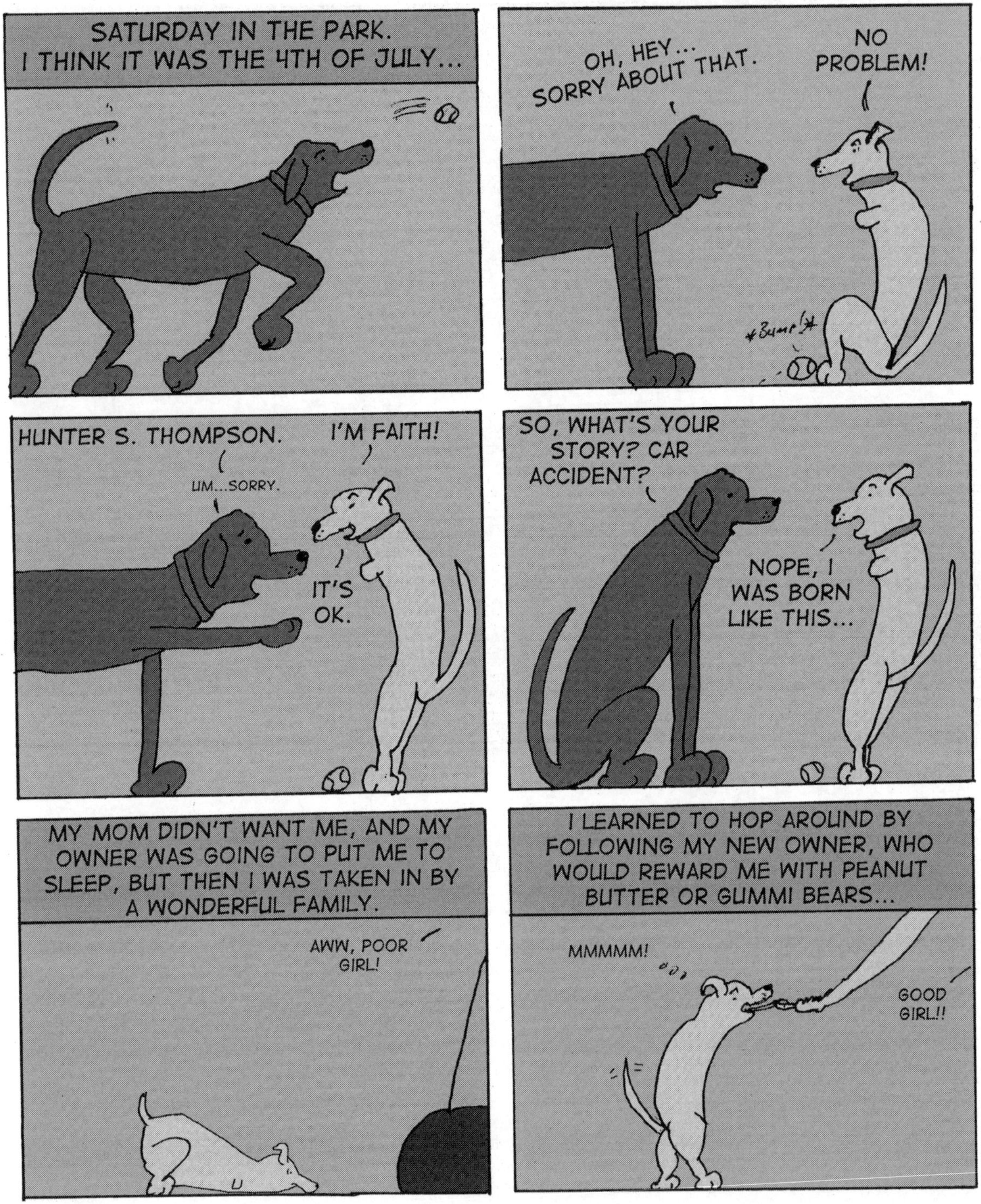
SATURDAY IN THE PARK.
I THINK IT WAS THE 4TH OF JULY...
OH, HEY... SORRY ABOUT THAT.
NO PROBLEM!
HUNTER S. THOMPSON.
UM...SORRY.
I'M FAITH!
IT'S OK.
SO, WHAT'S YOUR STORY? CAR ACCIDENT?
NOPE, I WAS BORN LIKE THIS...
MY MOM DIDN'T WANT ME, AND MY OWNER WAS GOING TO PUT ME TO SLEEP, BUT THEN I WAS TAKEN IN BY A WONDERFUL FAMILY.
AWW, POOR GIRL!
I LEARNED TO HOP AROUND BY FOLLOWING MY NEW OWNER, WHO WOULD REWARD ME WITH PEANUT BUTTER OR GUMMI BEARS...
MMMMM!
GOOD GIRL!!

A reader sent me the story of Faith, a dog born without her front legs and almost died before learning to walk on her hind legs. I just had to do a strip about her.

Check out faiththedog.info for more about this inspiring dog!

More Monday strips during "Bark To The Future" before I cut back my schedule three days a week. I had meant to get Boris out of the closet for a while, but never got around to it. I missed that little guy.

I'm a big fan of Zorphbert and Fred, a fantastic comic on the web by Dawn Griffin. I had an idea for a short little story involving Boris and Frohike, and wanted to use them for it. A quick e-mail later, Dawn gave me permission to use them in my strip, and I had a blast drawing them. So much so, that I've done three guest strips over at Z&F since then. You'll see one later in this book, and be sure to check out all the great comics at http://zfcomics.com

For those not familiar with them, Zorphbert and Fred are two aliens sent to earth to study humans while disguised as dogs. Zorphbert is the serious one, Fred is a little more fun loving. He wears an old sock as his "kitty tail", since he would prefer to be a cat. We've never seen them out of their suits, but occasionally they whip out a tentacle, which I was just dying to draw. Thanks again for letting me use your dogs, er, aliens, Dawn!

ZORPHBERT AND FRED APPEAR WITH PERMISSION AND ARE ©2007-2011 DAWN GRIFFIN. THANKS, DAWN! ZFCOMICS.COM

Frohike's got a good point. I might have to get me some tin foil.

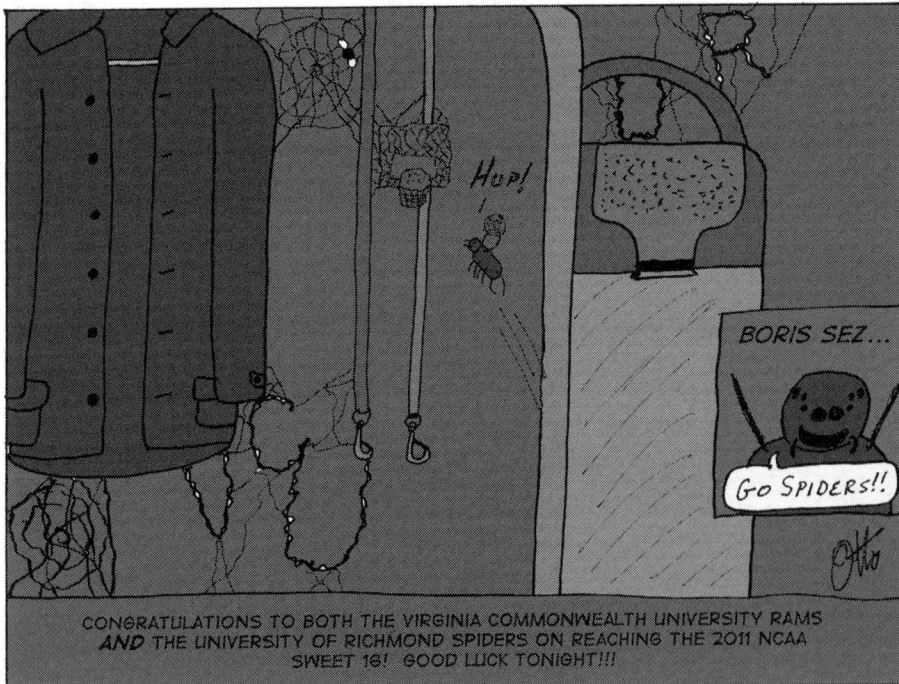

In March of 2011, two basketball teams from here in Richmond, Virginia made it into the sweet 16 of the men's NCAA tournament, the University of Richmond Spiders and the Virginia Commonwealth University Rams. The Rams went on to the final four, a real Cinderella story. A friend at work suggested I draw up something for it, and I came up with this sketch of Boris playing while he was stuck in the closet. Of course, he rooted for the Spiders.

Every week on Facebook, 1-800-Petmeds holds a trivia contest where the prize is a year's worth of Frontline. I won, and when they contacted me about permission to use my name for promotional things on their blog, I offered to draw up a comic, and they loved the idea! I drew this up and it was featured on their blog for a couple of days. The toy they sent also lasted a couple of days. Hunter likes to tear up stuffed toys.

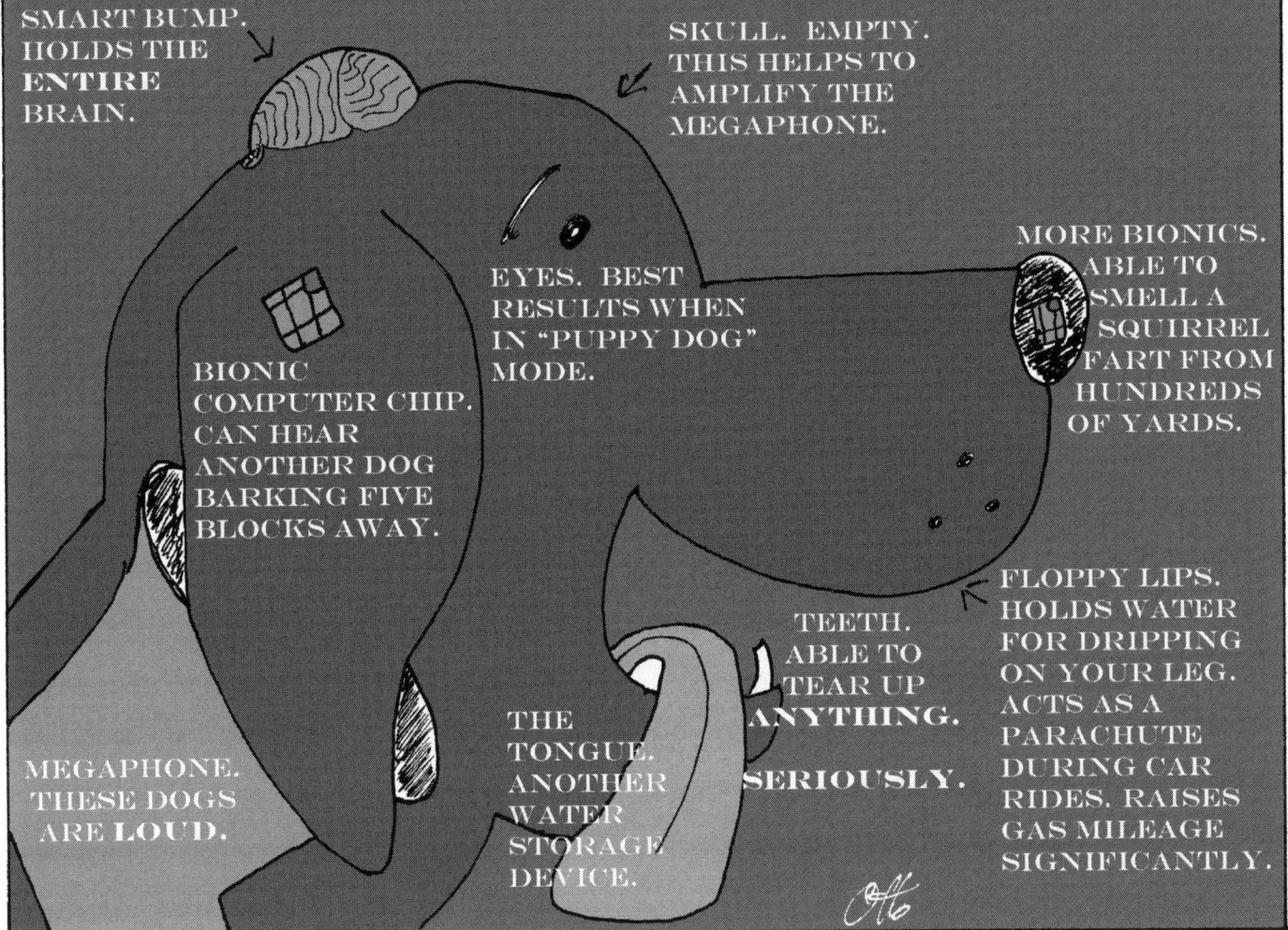

Before I started drawing comics, I sat down and brainstormed for a while to come up with a few stories. One thing I came up with was "Lab Anatomy", which resulted in these two sketches.

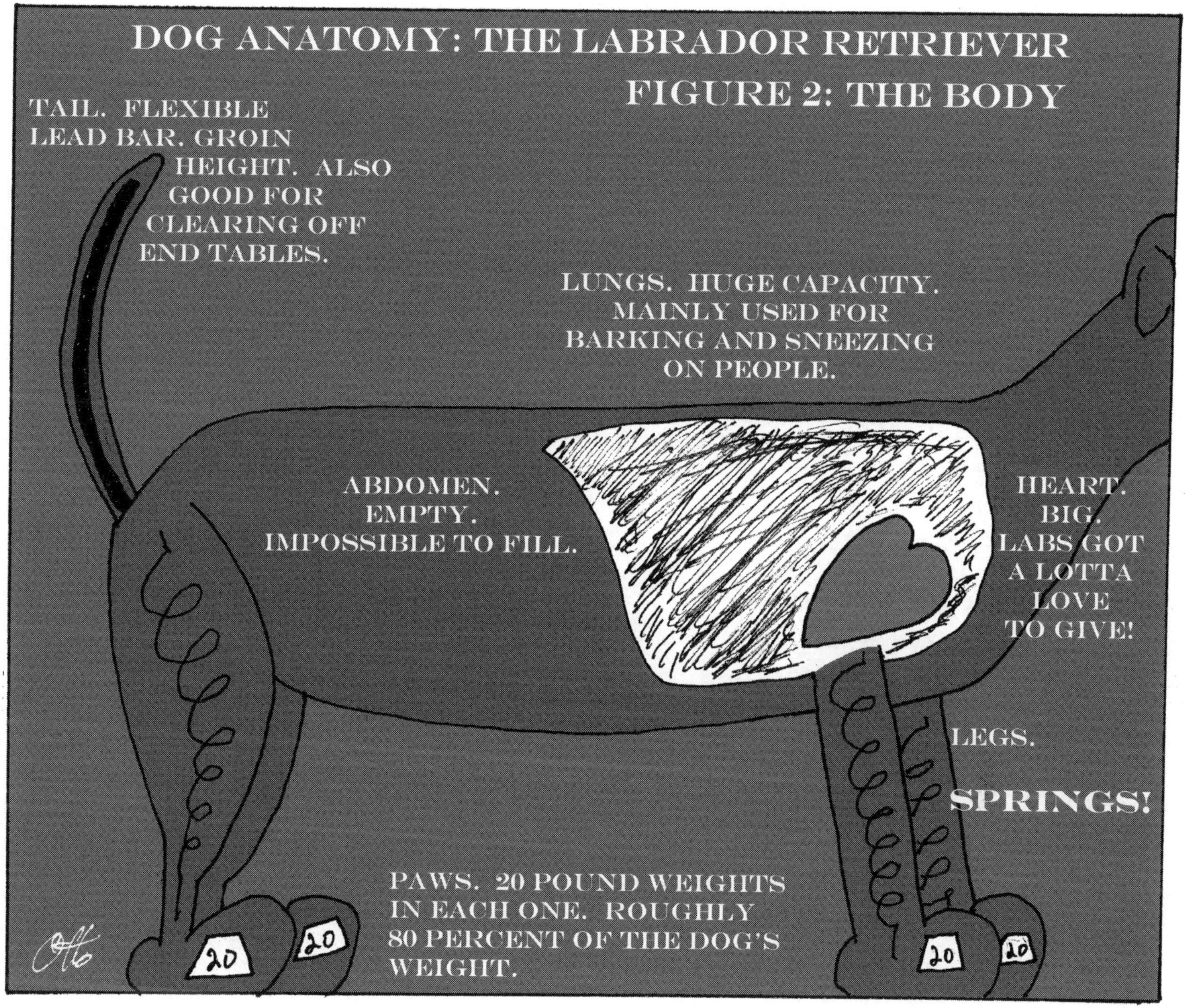
DOG ANATOMY: THE LABRADOR RETRIEVER
FIGURE 2: THE BODY
TAIL. FLEXIBLE LEAD BAR. GROIN HEIGHT. ALSO GOOD FOR CLEARING OFF END TABLES.
LUNGS. HUGE CAPACITY. MAINLY USED FOR BARKING AND SNEEZING ON PEOPLE.
ABDOMEN. EMPTY. IMPOSSIBLE TO FILL.
HEART. BIG. LABS GOT A LOTTA LOVE TO GIVE!
LEGS.
SPRINGS!
PAWS. 20 POUND WEIGHTS IN EACH ONE. ROUGHLY 80 PERCENT OF THE DOG'S WEIGHT.
20
20
20
20

Panel 1: HEY THERE, FOLKS! MY NAME IS HUNTER, AND I'M HERE TO TELL YOU HOW *GREAT* IT IS TO BE A DOG IN RICHMOND!

Panel 2: THERE ARE LOTS OF PARKS TO VISIT! ONE OF MY FAVORITES IS "BARKER FIELD" AT BYRD PARK.

NO LEASHES!

Panel 3: TWICE A SEASON THE FLYING SQUIRRELS INVITE ALL DOGS TO THE DIAMOND FOR "BARK IN THE PARK"!

HAVE *FUNN*, PUPS!

NUTZY IS A TM OF THE RICHMOND FLYING SQUIRRELS.

Panel 4: SWIMMING IN THE JAMES RIVER IS A GREAT SUMMER TREAT FOR ANY DOG WHO LOVES THE WATER.

Side text: I entered this comic into a contest for a local paper's annual comic issue. It was not printed, so I ran it on my site, along with a little rant, which I won't reprint here, but you can find it on my website.

Panel 5: RICHMOND IS ALSO A GREAT PLACE TO FIND A DOG OF YOUR OWN! THERE ARE LOTS OF LOCAL ADOPTION AGENCIES, AND YOU CAN VOLUNTEER TO HELP WALK AND FEED DOGS AND CATS AT SHELTERS IF YOU CAN'T HAVE A PET OF YOUR OWN.

OUR FOLKS GOT ME FROM AARF!

Panel 6: I'M *SO* GLAD TO BE A RICHMOND DOG! ANYTHING TO ADD, GILLIAN?

THERE'S TONS OF FUN THINGS FOR OUR PEOPLE TO DO HERE TOO! I DON'T KNOW WHERE TO BEGIN!

TRY *STYLEWEEKLY.COM!*

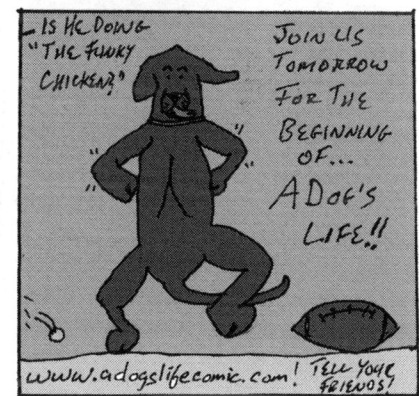

Not the first comic I drew, but it is the first comic I posted. It didn't really fit into my planned stories in the first couple of months, so I decided to post it the day before my "official" launch and call it #0. I know the whole "dogs versus Mike Vick" thing has been done tons, but I felt like taking my own shot at it.

Every time snow is in the forecast here in Richmond, the stores all sell out of milk, bread, and eggs. It's gotta be french toast.

Fun Fact! Jack's ringtone is from "All These Things That I've Done" by the Killers. I love that song.

This was something I envisioned being a semi-regular thing; home improvement tips that revolve around your dog. To date, this is the only one I have come up with. As I mentioned earlier, this is one of the few times I broke the 4th wall; I pictured Jack hosting his own home improvement show, but no one else can see it, hence Diane asking "who are you talking to?"

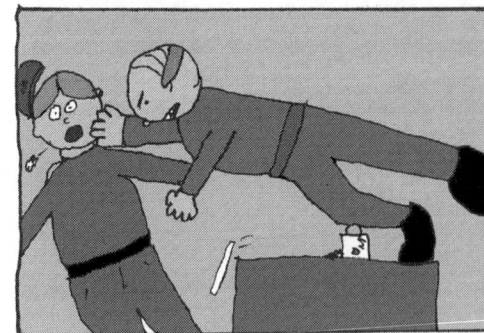

I occasionally feel like certain people should be slapped. I think we all do, really. I certainly never would, but *man*, some people deserve it. I've done a few strips about these situations, but I haven't done one in a while, because I thought that it might not be a great idea for a kid friendly strip to promote slapping stupid people.

This one is based on an article I saw in the New York Times. Many crimes in New York City are perpetrated by people wearing Yankee hats, therefore anyone wearing a Yankee hat is likely a criminal. That was the gist of the article.

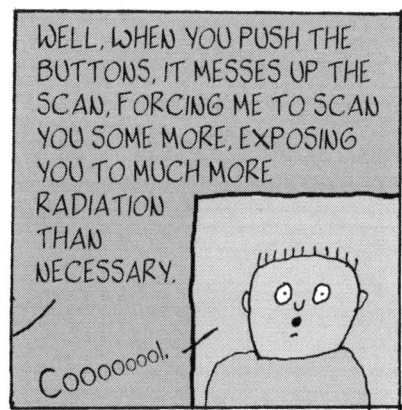

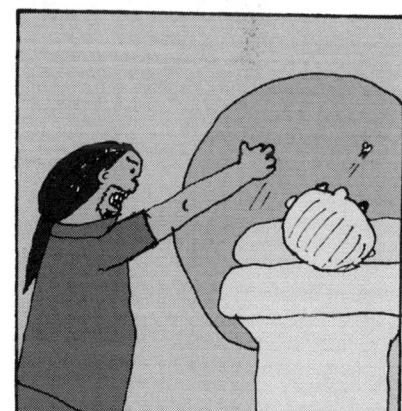

This one is based on a true story. I work as a CT technologist to pay the bills and support this cartooning thing. One night some guy was pushing the buttons on the machine. We didn't get into the whole superhero thing, but he did continue to push the buttons after I told him not to. He really did say, "I thought I was done," which I guess meant he could mess with the buttons some more.

This one is also based in truth. We've finally gotten a certain company to stop calling us with offers for TV packages despite the fact we told them several times that we were not interested. After being told it took 30 days to get off the calling list and then getting more calls more than a month later, I came up with the idea for this strip.

I left this strip hand lettered so you could get an idea as to why I stopped hand lettering strips. I think this was actually the first one I posted with the hand lettering.

STORMTROOPERS ARE A COPYRIGHT OF LUCASFILM LTD.

Another recurring strip idea, one that I plan to continue semi-regularly. It's no secret that I'm a **huge** fan of the Star Wars films. There are tons of scenes that lead you imagine what happens next. I like coming up with "deleted scenes", filling in the blanks.

In "The Empire Strikes Back" during the carbon freezing scene, Chewbacca flips out and starts hucking stormtroopers all over the place. When Boba Fett gets ready to shoot him, Darth Vader stops him. That always bugged me. Why the heck would Vader stop Fett? I have a theory. This is it.

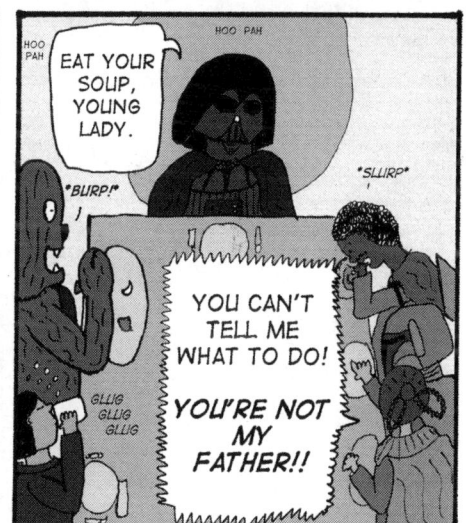

Another one from "Empire". Ever wonder what happens after Lando Calrissian betrays his friends and Darth Vader "invites" them to dinner? Me too. That had to be one *awkward* meal.

When Lucas released the Star Wars films on Blu-Ray, there were even more "enhancements" to the films added. I haven't seen them personally, but one that I heard about is the addition of Darth Vader screaming "NOOOOOO!" when he chucks the Emperor down the reactor shaft. I wondered if there might be some other times where Vader would have a reason to belt out a hearty "NOOOOOOOOO!!!" Plus, when the phrase "Ewok in a Wok" popped into my head, it just had to be drawn.

I wanted to do something special for my 200th comic posted. I thought it'd be neat to post every single one of them. It took a long time to paste together, but I thought the end result was totally worth it.

If you look very closely, you can see a few of the strips from the epic story, "Bark To The Future", written by my friend Ben Taylor and drawn by myself. They will be printed in their own separate collection, as it is more than 150 strips long! I'm not kidding when I say "epic".

That's it for my comics! The rest of the book is guest strips I've done for other sites, some con sketches, and a couple of other tidbits. Enjoy!

©2011 ADOGSLIFECOMIC.COM

I've had the opportunity to have guest strips I've done posted on two of my favorite comics on the web; Zorphbert and Fred by Dawn Griffin, and Capes & Babes by Chris Flick. I've had he opportunity to meet both Dawn and Chris in person at conventions, and they are both just as cool as they are talented, which is a lot!

CAPES & BABES BY CHRIS FLICK

SOOKIE, BILL, TRU-BLOOD AND MERLOTTE'S © HBO

This was my first guest strip! Capes & Babes is a hilarious comic about a strip mall, a comic book shop, and one *crazy* werewolf. Roy is the werewolf, and he's dating Roni, a vampire. I thought it'd be fun to drop them into the world of HBO's "True Blood". When it posted, Chris added a bit to it, turning me into a reporter for the WWN, (Weird World News) and even drawing me into the strip. Thanks, Chris!

http://www.capesnbabes.com/2011/05/13/546-weird-world-news-chris-otto-guest-strip/

Be sure to check out all the great comics at www.capesnbabes.com

When Dawn took a month off to build up a buffer and revamp her comic a bit in October 2011, she put out a request for guest art and strips. I had so much fun drawing them in my strip, I had to jump at the chance to draw them again. I came up with a fun idea, and got to make more "X-Files" jokes!

http://www.zfcomics.com/comics/bufferotto/

Check out all of Dawn's great work at www.zfcomics.com

This was a piece of fan art I did for Danielle Corsetto, who does the online comic "Girls With Slingshots". The cats in this piece are from her comic. Special Kitty (complete with braces) on the left, and Ghost Kitty on the right. Check out her fantastic strip at www.girlswithslingshots.com (not for kids, folks!)

This is kind of embarrassing, and I almost didn't include it here, but this is actually the **VERY** first comic I drew. After I decided to start up a comic, I drove up to the Small Press Expo in Bethesda, Maryland in early September, 2010, to buy "How To Make Webcomics" from my idol, Dave Kellett. I brought this with me to give him. It's what might happen if my comic dog, Hunter, met his comic dog, Oso (a pug). Check out Dave's wonderful strip, "Sheldon" at www.sheldoncomics.com

Without Sheldon, I probably would never had the desire to start my own comic. I want to make a strip that makes others as happy as his makes me when I read it.

I was fortunate enough to make some amazing friends (including "Bark To The Future" writer Ben Taylor) at the Virginia Comicon in November of 2010 when I went as a volunteer to see what conventions were like and to get my foot in the door by ingratiating myself to the folks who run it by helping out some. I've had a table at pretty much every one since then, as well as the DC Comicon in June 2011. Thanks to Brett Carreras for giving me a shot! Here are a few sketches from the DC Con.

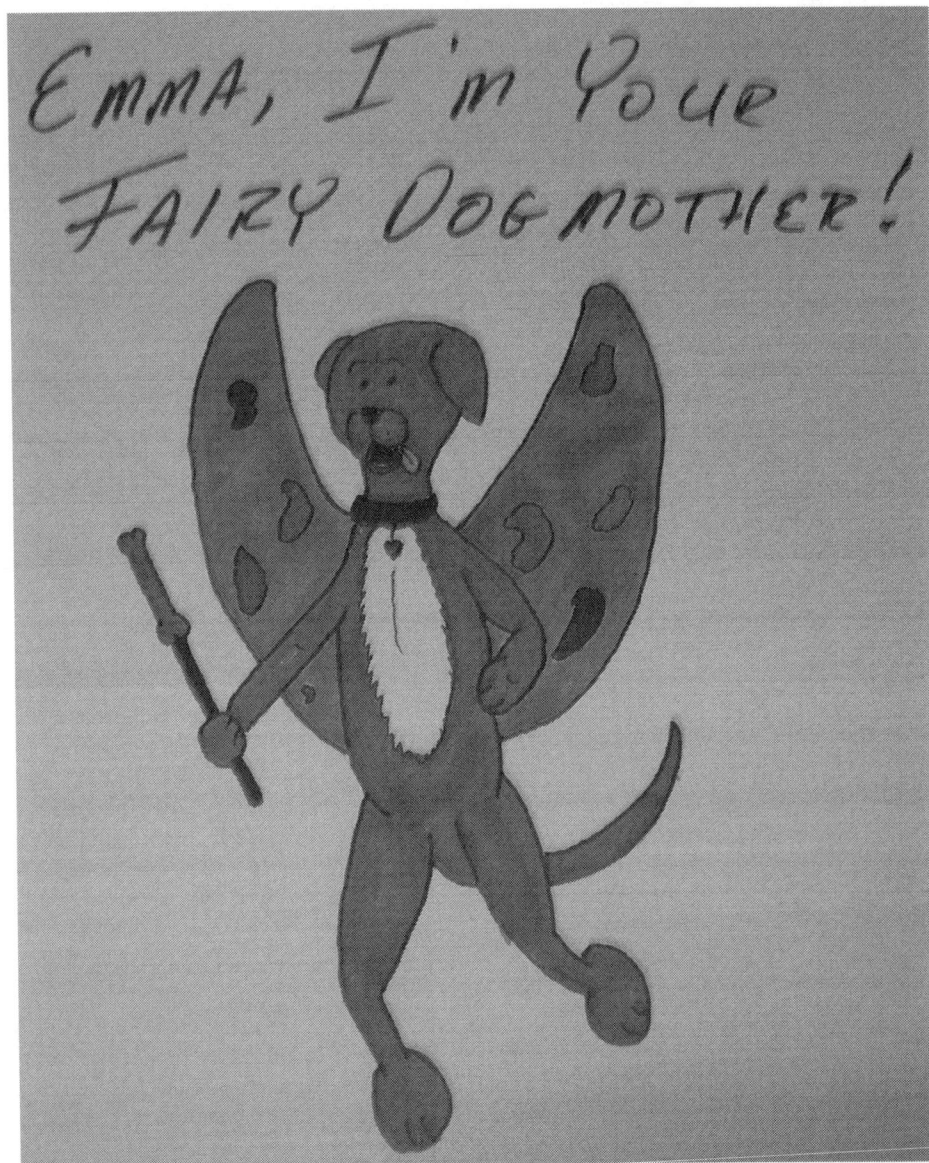

EMMA, I'M YOUR FAIRY DOGMOTHER!

Emma wanted me to draw her a princess, but since people are not really my strong point, her mom and I talked her down to a fairy. This is basically Gillian with wings, but she was happy and happy kids make me happy!

A fun mash up of the Road Runner as the Golden Age Flash. This was my first real commissioned sketch for a con regular who comes up with some real fun mash up ideas. I am honored to be a part of his Golden Age Looney Tunes collection. It's also the first sketch I did that wasn't a dog.

Dogs drawn as super heroes (or villains) has become my main sketching style. Since I do a comic about dogs, and don't really draw people very well, that makes sense, right? Here are Cyclops from the X-Men (above) and K-9 America (left). I often try to come up with punny names for the sketches. You'll also notice that cats are tormented fairly regularly in them as well.

THE FANTASTIC FUR!

I did a bunch of sketches with colored pencils as I geared up to start doing conventions. This was one of my first ones...the Fantastic Fur!

Wooferine and Shadowcat! One of the few times I'll draw a cat as a hero, not a victim. My wife colored this one for me. She's a much better colorist than I am.

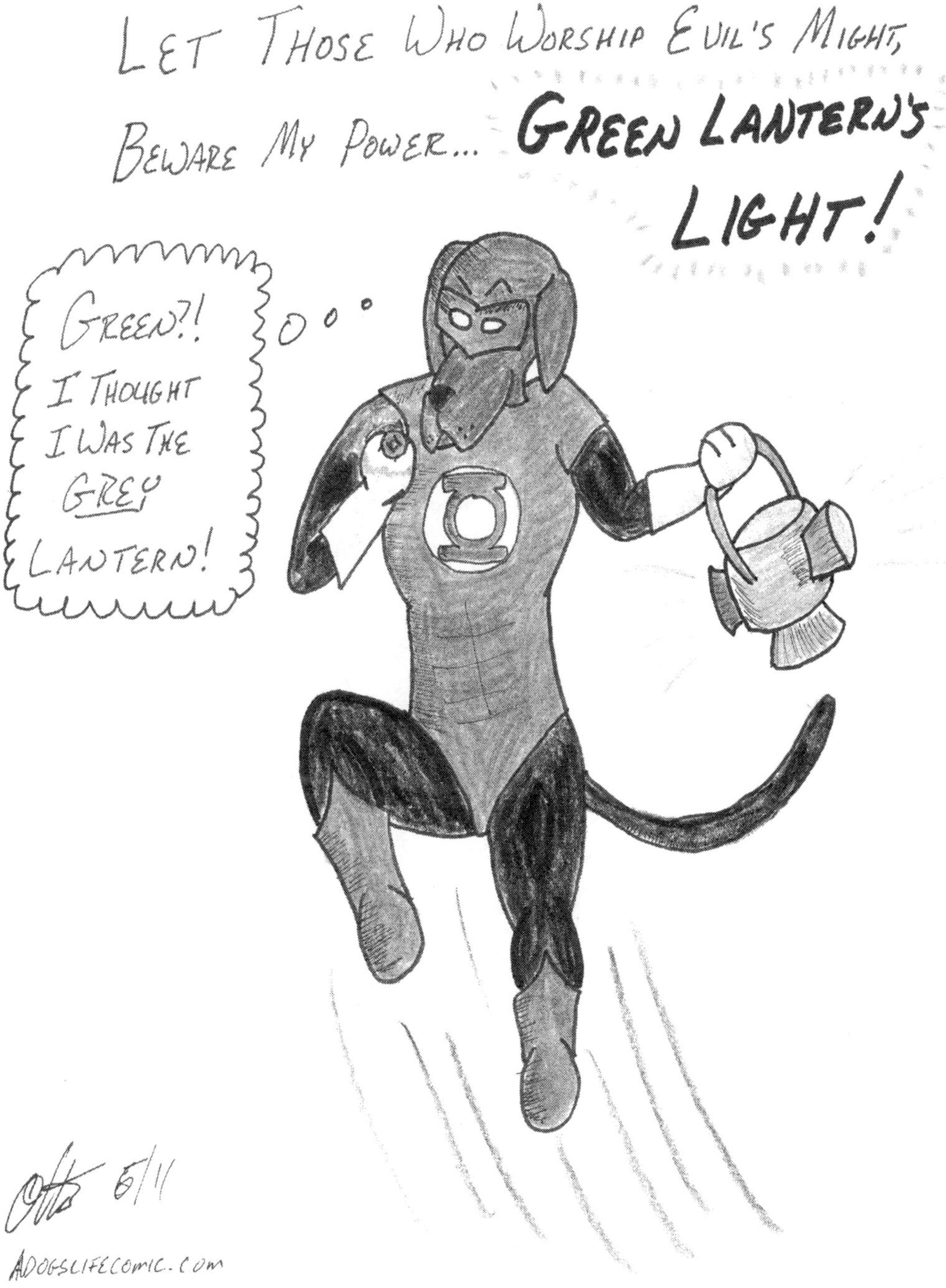
LET THOSE WHO WORSHIP EVIL'S MIGHT,
BEWARE MY POWER... GREEN LANTERN'S LIGHT!
GREEN?! I THOUGHT I WAS THE GREY LANTERN!
ADOGSLIFECOMIC.COM

Get it? Dogs are color blind!

I crack myself up.

Spider-Dog! I had fun basing the sign in the background on the failed Spider-man Broadway show, "Turn Off The Dark".

I meant to put "Turn Off The Bark" on the sign.

WOOFERINE

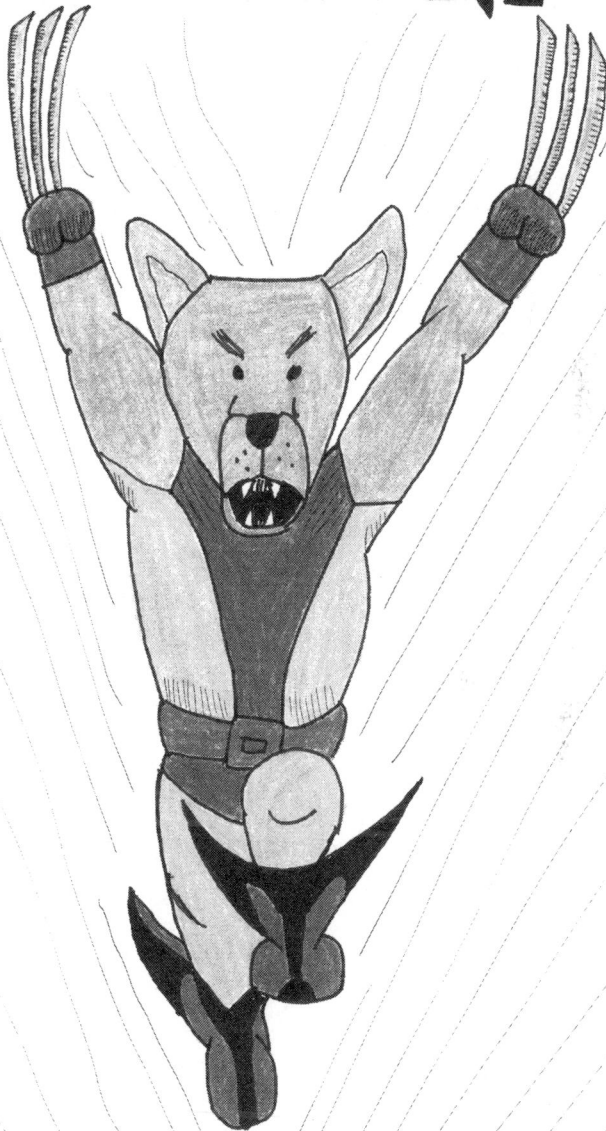

Another Wooferine. I did
quite a few of these.

I'm a big fan of Doctor Who, and it was only logical to draw up some "Dogtor Who" sketches. If you're not a fan of Doctor Who, you're missing out. The Ood (that's the alien) fry people with those glowy balls they carry around. I thought this one was pretty funny!

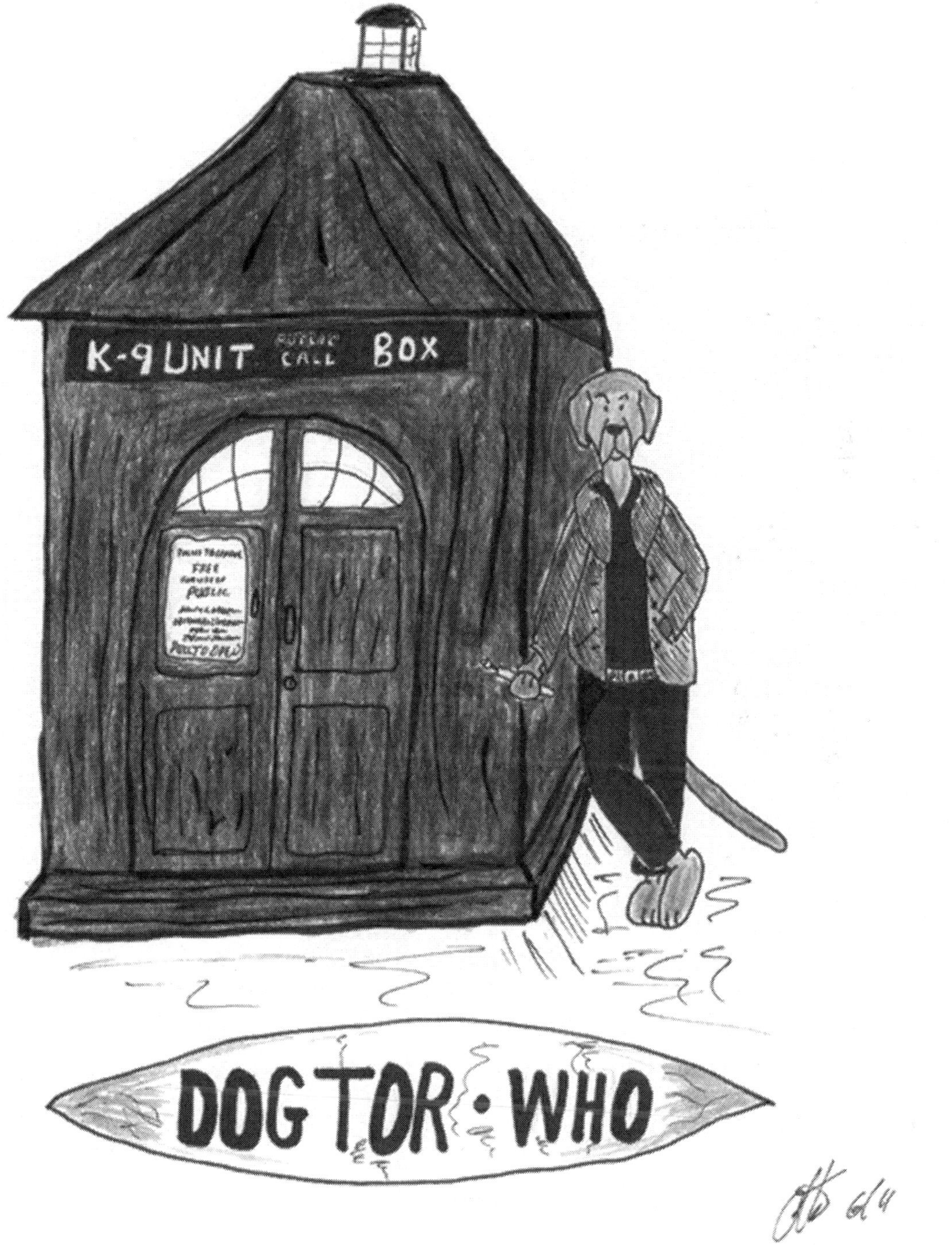
K-9 UNIT
CALL
BOX
DOGTOR • WHO

And, of course, being a massive Star Wars fan, I've done a few based on them as well. Arf Vader is one of my favorites.

Luke Dogwalker Battles Arf Vader!

Boba Fetch is another one that's fun to draw.

HOW TO DRAW HUNTER S. THOMPSON
(THE DOG, NOT THE WRITER)

STEP 1: THE NOSE

BASICALLY A ROUNDED TRIANGLE.

THE CURVE IS USED TO
CHANGE HUNTER'S MOOD.
UP FOR SMILING, DOWN
FOR ANGRY OR UNHAPPY.

STEP 2: THE SNOUT

HUNTER HAS FLOPPY LIPS.

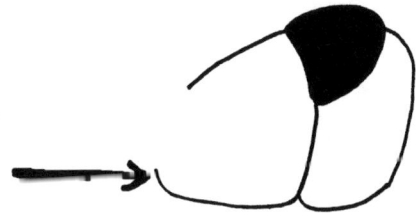

STEP 3: THE MOUTH

THE FRONT COMES OFF THE MIDDLE
OF THE SNOUT. DRAW THE TONGUE,
FILL IN THE MOUTH, THEN DRAW THE
JAW CURVING AROUND THE MOUTH.

STEP 4: THE EAR
ALONG WITH THE FLOPPY LIPS,
HUNTER HAS BIG, FLOPPY EARS.

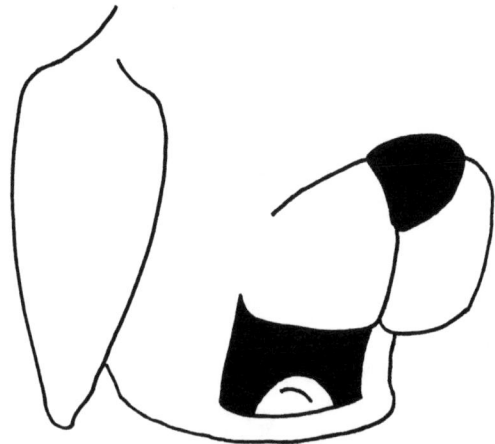

I OFTEN CHANGE THE EAR TO
MATCH HUNTER'S MOOD; PERKY,
NORMAL, OR HANGING LOW
WHEN HE'S UPSET.

STEP 5: THE HEAD
THE SMART BUMP COMES OFF THE TOP OF THE EAR, THEN HIS BROW CURVES AROUND TO THE MIDDLE OF THE NOSE. THEN ADD THE LEFT EAR.

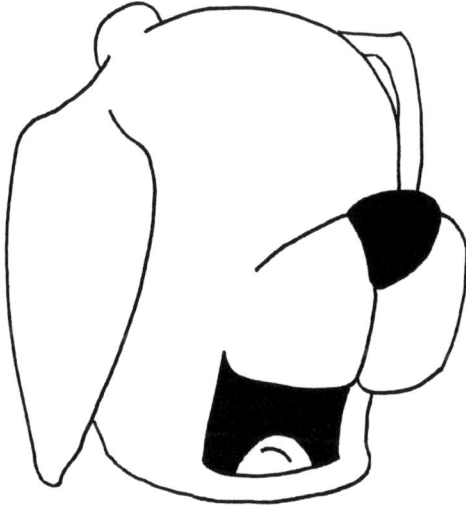

STEP 6: FACIAL DETAILS
ADD THE EYES, EYEBROWS, AND THREE WHISKERS ON EACH SIDE OF HIS SNOUT.

STEP 7: THE NECK

THE BACK OF THE NECK COMES OFF THE MIDDLE OF THE EAR. THE FRONT LINES UP WITH THE BACK OF THE TONGUE. ADD THE COLLAR LAST.

STEP 8: WITTY DIALOGUE

ADD A WORD BALLOON WITH SOME CLEVER JOKE. THIS IS THE HARDEST PART.

I LIKE FETCH!

What Might Have Been....

I've often lamented that I started posting comics too soon, and that I should have practiced my drawing a lot more before I got going. Just for giggles, I thought I would re-draw one of my early strips for the book, just to see what those comics could have looked like. This is one of my favorite early strips!

I hope you enjoyed my first book! Thank you so much for purchasing it! Share it with your friends! I hope you continue following the shenanigans of Hunter, Gillian, and everyone else, on the web at http://adogslifecomic.com

THANKS FOR READING "A DOG'S LIFE!"

51750048R00076

Made in the USA
Charleston, SC
03 February 2016